The Brick Testament

The Story of Christmas

Library of Congress Cataloging in Publication Number: 2004102136

ISBN: 1-59474-012-7

Printed in Singapore

Typeset in Agincourt, Edwardian Medium, and Goudy

Designed by Andrea Stephany

Distributed in North America by Chronicle Books
85 Second Street
San Francisco, CA 94105

10 9 8 7 6 5 4 3 2 1

Quirk Books
215 Church Street
Philadelphia, PA 19106
www.quirkbooks.com

The Brick Testament

The Story of Christmas

Retold and Illustrated by Brendan Powell Smith

QUIRK BOOKS

PHILADELPHIA

𝕿his is how Jesus Christ came to be born.

Mt 1:18

God sent the angel Gabriel to a town in Galilee

called Nazareth . . .

Lk 1:26

. . . to a virgin betrothed to a man named Joseph,

who was descended from King David.

The virgin's name was Mary.

LK 1:27

The angel came to her and said,

"Greetings, highly favored one!

The Lord is with you."

Lk 1:28

Mary was greatly troubled by his words,

and wondered what this sort of greeting might mean.

Lᴋ 1:29

𝕿he angel said to her, "Listen!

You will conceive in your womb and bear a son.

You will name him Jesus."

Lk 1:30–31

Mary said to the angel,

"How can this happen if I am a virgin?"

Lk 1:34

$\mathfrak{T}$he angel answered,

"The Holy Ghost will come upon you."

Lᴋ 1:35

And the angel left her.

Lk 1:38

Shortly afterward, Mary got up and
hurried off to the hill country.

Lk 1:39

$\mathfrak{S}$he entered the house of Zechariah the priest

and greeted his wife, Elizabeth.

Mary said, "My soul exalts the Lord in praise!"

Lk 1:40, 46

"He has wrought mighty deeds with his arm.

He has scattered the proud and arrogant."

Lᴋ 1:51

"He has cast down rulers from their thrones."

Lk 1:52

"*And* has raised up the lowly."

Lk 1:52

$\mathfrak{M}$ary remained with Elizabeth

for about three months,

and then returned home.

Lk 1:56

𝕸ary was found to be with child of the Holy Ghost.

MT 1:18

Being an upright man,

and not wanting to disgrace her in public,

Joseph had decided to leave Mary quietly.

Mt 1:19

But as he considered this, an angel of the Lord

appeared to him in a dream, saying,

"Joseph, do not be afraid to take Mary as your wife.

The child in her is of the Holy Ghost.

She will give birth to a son.

You will name him Jesus."

Mt 1:20–21

About this time, Caesar Augustus ordered a census of the entire Roman Empire, and so everyone went to their own towns to be registered. Because he was a descendant of King David, Joseph set out from Nazareth to the town of David, called Bethlehem, to register with Mary, his betrothed.

LK 2:1, 3–5

While they were there,

the time came for Mary to deliver her child,

and she gave birth to her firstborn son.

Lk 2:6–7

She wrapped him in bands of cloth,

and laid him in a manger,

because there was no room for them at the inn.

L<small>K</small> 2:7

44

There were some shepherds out in the nearby fields,

keeping watch over their flock at night.

Lk 2:8

An angel of the Lord appeared before them,

and the glory of the Lord shone around them.

The shepherds were terrified.

Lk 2:9

But the angel said, "Don't be afraid!

Listen, a Savior has been born to you today

who is Christ the Lord. Here is your sign:

you will find a baby wrapped in strips of cloth,

lying in a manger."

Lk 2:10–12

$\mathfrak{S}$uddenly, a multitude of the heavenly host

was there with the angel, praising God and saying,

"Glory to God in the highest, and on earth

peace among men he favors."

Lk 2:13–14

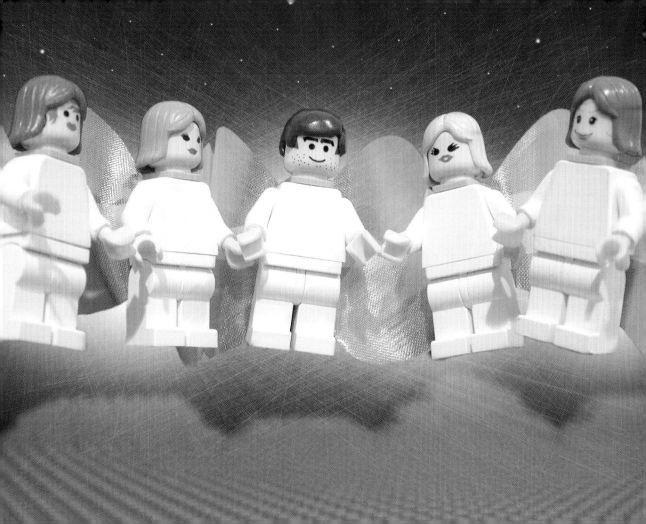

So the shepherds left in a hurry.

Lk 2:16

$\mathfrak{A}$nd they found Mary and Joseph,

and the baby was lying in the manger.

Lk 2:16

Having seen the baby, the shepherds made known

what they had been told about this child.

All who heard the news marveled at the things

the shepherds told them.

Lk 2:17–18

58

𝔄fter eight days passed,

it was time for the child to be circumcised.

He was given the name Jesus.

Lk 2:21

60

*A*fter Jesus was born, some magi

from the east came to Jerusalem, saying,

"Where is he who is born King of the Jews?

For we saw his star when it rose,

and have come to do him homage."

Mt 2:1–2

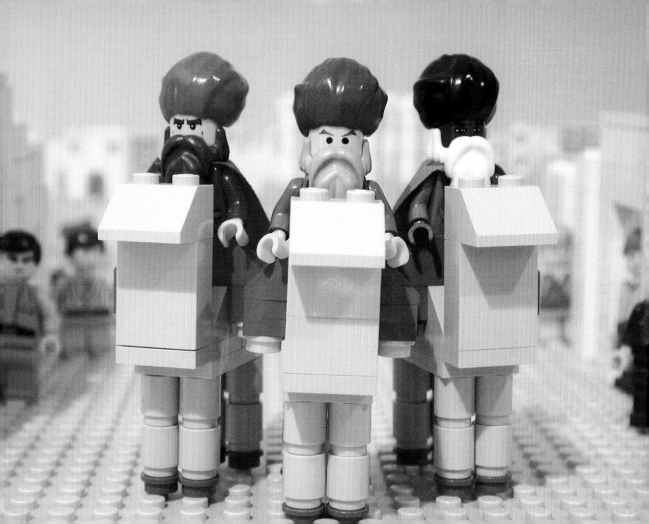

When Herod the king heard about this,

he was disturbed, as was all of Jerusalem with him.

Mt 2:3

Gathering together all the chief priests and experts
on the Law of Moses, King Herod asked them
where the Messiah was to be born. They said to him,
"At Bethlehem in Judea, just as it was written
by the prophet."

MT 2:4–5

66

Then King Herod summoned the magi.

He sent them off to Bethlehem, saying,

"Go and search for the young child.

When you have found him, let me know,

so that I may also go and do him homage."

MT 2:7–8

Having listened to the king, the magi set off. The star that they had seen rising went on before them until it came to a stop over the place where the child was.

Mt 2:9–10

𝕿hey came into the house

and saw the young child with his mother, Mary.

MT 2:11

They bowed down and did him homage.

Opening their treasures, they offered gifts

of gold, frankincense, and myrrh.

But the magi were warned in a dream

that they should not return to King Herod,

and so they traveled back to their own country

by a different route.

Mt 2:12

After the magi had left, an angel of the Lord appeared to Joseph in a dream and said, "Get up and take the child and his mother. Flee into Egypt. Stay there until I tell you, for King Herod will be searching for the child to destroy him."

MT 2:13

Joseph got up that night

and took the child and his mother,

and went to Egypt.

Mt 2:14

When King Herod realized

that he had been tricked by the magi,

he was furious.

Mt 2:16

He sent out soldiers to kill all the male children

two years old or younger throughout Bethlehem

and the surrounding countryside.

MT 2:16

After King Herod died, an angel of the Lord

appeared to Joseph in a dream, saying,

"Get up and take the child and his mother.

Go to the land of Israel, for those

who sought to kill the child are dead."

Mt 2:19–20

Joseph got up and took the child and his mother,

and returned to the land of Israel.

MT 2:21

But when he heard that Archelaus,

the son of King Herod, was reigning over Judea,

Joseph was afraid to go there.

Then being warned by God in a dream,

he withdrew to the region of Galilee

and came to live in a town called Nazareth.

Mt 2:22

𝕿he child grew

and became strong and filled with wisdom.

And God's favor was with him.

Lᴋ 2:40

$\mathcal{A}$nd that is the story of Christmas.

THE END

About the Author

The second son of a Sunday school superintendent, the self-styled "Reverend"
Brendan Powell Smith has spent the past three years illustrating more than
one hundred stories from the Bible with LEGO® bricks. His work has appeared
in several national and international magazines and newspapers including
Time, *People*, *Entertainment Weekly*, *SPIN*, *Church Times*, and *Bible Review*.

Smith is also the author of *The Brick Testament: Stories from the Book of Genesis*.
More of his work can be seen on the Internet at www.thebricktestament.com

"Reverend" Brendan Powell Smith